50

SPORTS GREAT JOHN STOCKTON

—*Sports Great Books* —

Sports Great Jim Abbott
(ISBN 0-89490-395-0)

Sports Great Troy Aikman
(ISBN 0-89490-593-7)

Sports Great Charles Barkley
(ISBN 0-89490-386-1)

Sports Great Larry Bird
(ISBN 0-89490-368-3)

Sports Great Barry Bonds
(ISBN 0-89490-595-3)

Sports Great Bobby Bonilla
(ISBN 0-89490-417-5)

Sports Great Will Clark
(ISBN 0-89490-390-X)

Sports Great Roger Clemens
(ISBN 0-89490-284-9)

Sports Great John Elway
(ISBN 0-89490-282-2)

Sports Great Patrick Ewing
(ISBN 0-89490-369-1)

Sports Great Steffi Graf
(ISBN 0-89490-597-X)

Sports Great Orel Hershiser
(ISBN 0-89490-389-6)

Sports Great Bo Jackson
(ISBN 0-89490-281-4)

**Sports Great Magic Johnson
(Revised and Expanded)**
(ISBN 0-89490-348-9)

Sports Great Michael Jordan
(ISBN 0-89490-370-5)

Sports Great Mario Lemieux
(ISBN 0-89490-596-1)

Sports Great Karl Malone
(ISBN 0-89490-599-6)

Sports Great Kevin Mitchell
(ISBN 0-89490-388-8)

Sports Great Joe Montana
(ISBN 0-89490-371-3)

Sports Great Hakeem Olajuwon
(ISBN 0-89490-372-1)

Sports Great Shaquille O'Neal
(ISBN 0-89490-594-5)

Sports Great Kirby Puckett
(ISBN 0-89490-392-6)

Sports Great Jerry Rice
(ISBN 0-89490-419-1)

Sports Great Cal Ripken, Jr.
(ISBN 0-89490-387-X)

Sports Great David Robinson
(ISBN 0-89490-373-X)

Sports Great Nolan Ryan
(ISBN 0-89490-394-2)

Sports Great Barry Sanders
(ISBN 0-89490-418-3)

Sports Great John Stockton
(ISBN 0-89490-598-8)

Sports Great Darryl Strawberry
(ISBN 0-89490-291-1)

Sports Great Isiah Thomas
(ISBN 0-89490-374-8)

Sports Great Herschel Walker
(ISBN 0-89490-207-5)

SPORTS GREAT JOHN STOCKTON

Nathan Aaseng

—Sports Great Books—

ENSLOW PUBLISHERS, INC.
44 Fadem Road   P.O. Box 38
Box 699   Aldershot
Springfield, N.J. 07081   Hants GU12 6BP
U.S.A.   U.K.

Library of Congress Cataloging-in-Publication Data

Aaseng, Nathan.
    Sports great John Stockton / Nathan Aaseng.
        p. cm. — (Sports great books)
    Includes index.
    ISBN 0-89490-598-8
    1. Stockton, John, 1962- —Juvenile literature. 2. Basketball
players—United States—Biography—Juvenile literature. 3. National
Basketball Association—Juvenile literature. [1. Stockton,
John, 1962-   . 2. Basketball players.] I. Title. II. Series.
GV884.S76A27   1995
796.323'092–dc20
[B]
                                          94-34940
                                            CIP
                                            AC

Printed in the United States of America

10 9 8 7 6 5 4 3 2 1

Illustration Credits: Norm Perdue, pp. 8, 10, 24, 25, 29, 36, 39, 41, 45, 47, 48, 49, 54, 58,
60; Gary Dineen, pp. 15, 33; Courtesy of Gonzaga University, p. 17; Courtesy of the
University of Michigan, p. 22; Courtesy of Louisiana Tech University, p. 26.

Cover Illustration: Norm Perdue

Contents

Chapter 1

Even the casual basketball fan could tell that the 1984 National Basketball Association (NBA) draft of college players was no ordinary draft. That year, the colleges were turning loose a fleet of awesome athletes who could instantly pump up even the sorriest pro team. Michael Jordan, Hakeem Olajuwon, Kevin Willis, Sam Perkins, and Charles Barkley were just a few of the fine players ready to turn pro.

As the pro teams began announcing their draft choices in June 1984, more than five thousand fans in Utah jammed the Salt Palace. They eagerly awaited news of their team's choice. Utah's surprising Midwest Division championship in 1983-84 spurred dreams of even greater success. All week long, fans talked about which new player might bring them a step closer to an NBA title. Utah, however, had kept a tight lid on the secret of who it was they wanted to choose.

NBA teams drafted according to their won-lost records—those with the worst records chose first. That meant that Utah had to wait until the sixteenth choice before they could claim a player.

John Stockton had worried what fans of the Utah Jazz would think of the team's first draft pick—a six-foot one-inch guard from a little-known university.

Utah fans checked off each of the skywalking superstars as the bottom NBA teams claimed them. Houston chose Olajuwon, the Nigerian giant with the catlike reflexes. Chicago selected the College Player of the Year, Michael Jordan. Philadelphia claimed the ferocious Round Mound of Rebound, Charles Barkley. And so it went.

Finally, Utah's turn arrived. Fans leaned forward to catch the name of the new star. They heard "John Stockton, a six-foot one-inch guard from Gonzaga University."

No cheering or clapping arose from the Jazz fans. Nor was the Salt Palace buzzing with excitement. Instead, a murmur ran through the crowd. John Stockton was with Utah officials at the NBA draft headquarters in New York. He found a man who was speaking by phone to someone at the Salt Palace. Stockton knew the fans were hoping for a big-name star, and he feared the worst. "Are they booing?" he asked.

"They're not booing," he was told. "They're all asking, 'Who?'" Not only had many fans not heard of John Stockton, they had never heard of the school he played for—Gonzaga University.

It was only fitting that John Stockton should enter the NBA deep in the shadow of one of the most glamorous classes of rookies. Stockton was well used to the shadows. After all, he had played his college ball at a small school tucked away in the Pacific Northwest. Stockton was perfectly content to let others claim the spotlight, the headlines, the scoring titles, and the highlight films.

In a sport dominated by graceful giants, Stockton seemed out of place. At six feet one inch, he had to look up to almost everyone else in the league, and he stood a good foot shorter than many NBA centers. Stockton was not blessed with the acrobatic skills of most NBA stars. He was neither an

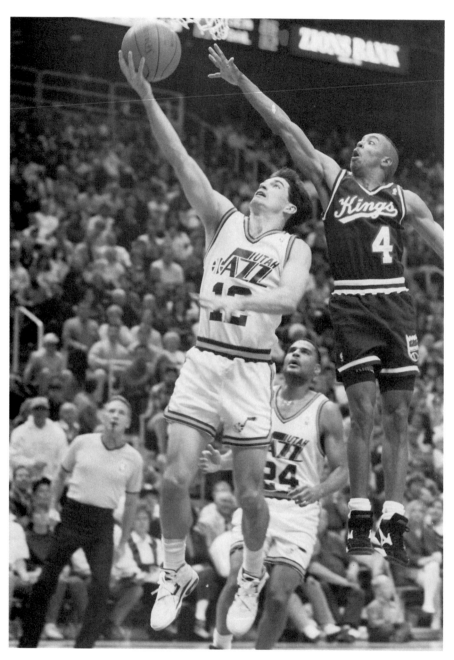

Stockton never let his size become an obstacle to an NBA career. Here Stockton takes advantage of a brief defensive lapse by the Sacramento Kings.

outstanding shooter, nor a kangaroo leaper. Crowd-pleasing slam dunks and 50-point scoring games were not his style.

In fact, Stockton's physical skills were so limited that, throughout most of his high school and college careers, no one thought of him as pro material. Many college coaches did not think he could compete even on the college level. Stockton's own family took a realistic view of the situation. According to Stockton's father, "The only person in the world who thought John would play in the NBA was John."

In writing off little John Stockton's chances of turning pro, observers ignored two important measurements: the size of a basketball court, and the size of Stockton's heart.

A pro basketball court is ninety-four feet long. Scoring statistics only take into account who guided the ball the last few feet into the basket. Talented scorers, however, are useless to a team that cannot move the ball across the rest of the court into scoring position. John Stockton may be better at taking care of the basketball than any other player who has ever lived. As long as Stockton has his hands on the ball, his team is almost always going to get a shot at the basket. Given Stockton's expert passing skills and unselfish play, that shot is likely to be a good one.

Basketball experts also underestimated Stockton's heart. John had always been a fierce competitor. He simply refused to give up on his dream of playing pro ball. If he failed, it would only be after he spent every last ounce of energy going for his goal.

Throughout Stockton's career, anyone who has ever played against him has trudged out of the gym a tired man. Stockton gives full effort all game, every game. As former teammate Kelly Tripucka said of him, "He's a nuisance and that's a compliment. He's like a fly that won't go out of the house."

So while Jordan, Olajuwon, and Barkley swooped and soared, and rebounded and scored on the NBA's center stage, Stockton quietly went about his business. He studied, and practiced, and learned, and improved. Stockton mastered Utah's offense. Almost unnoticed, he challenged and then succeeded the flashy Magic Johnson as the best floor general in the league.

In the 1990s, Stockton firmly established himself as the top player at his position in the NBA. In a 1994 survey by *Sports Illustrated*, NBA coaches overwhelmingly rated Stockton the league's best passer. "It's not even close," said one coach. "After him, there's a hole a mile wide."

Yet Stockton continues to shun the spotlight and to put team play ahead of personal glory. His best work remains almost invisible to the average fan. As a result, he remains one of the NBA's best-kept secrets despite a decade of record-shattering excellence. When Stockton's name comes up in a discussion of America's top sports stars, many people are still asking, "Who?"

Chapter 2

When John Stockton joined the NBA, he was as unfamiliar with most of the United States as fans were with him. Until he joined the Utah Jazz, he had spent virtually all his life within a few blocks of his first home.

John Houston Stockton was born on March 26, 1962, in Spokane, Washington, near the Idaho border. Although Spokane (Spo·CAN) was home to more than 100,000 people, it had a small-town feel for the Stocktons. Jack and Clementine Stockton raised John, his brother, and two sisters in a comfortable cocoon of security.

The family were devout Roman Catholics, surrounded by Catholic neighbors. John enrolled in the same three Catholic schools that his father had attended. For the first twenty-two years of his life, John required no transportation other than his feet to get where he needed to go. The schools, the church he attended regularly, and his father's place of employment were all located within easy walking distance of his home.

Jack Stockton provided a stable living as co-owner and operator of a bar that he bought shortly before John was born.

Business at "Jack & Dan's" was always good, helped by the fact that it was located just a block away from a college campus. With the bar just a 150-yard sprint down the block from the Stockton home, young John could regularly visit his dad at work. He could even stop by after school on his way home from St. Aloyisius Elementary School.

Jack Stockton installed a basketball hoop in the driveway of their home when the children were small. This became the arena for a keen rivalry between John and his brother, Steve. Steve was a fine athlete. As a high school pitcher, he once struck out crosstown rival Ryne Sandberg three times in a game. (Sandberg went on to an All-Star career with the Chicago Cubs.) Steve also played high school basketball, even though he grew no taller than five feet eight inches.

Both Stockton boys hated to lose. Even though he was four years older than John, Steve seldom took it easy on his kid brother. Little John had to scrap for the few points he could get. He learned to dive after loose balls and play hard on defense. The battles between the brothers were so intense that they left a lasting mark on John. The Stocktons get along well today. Yet, even after years of battling Michael Jordan, Magic Johnson, Charles Barkley, and Shaquille O'Neal, Stockton still says, "I can think of nobody I'd like to beat more than my brother."

Fueled by a desire to compete with his older brother, John practically lived on the basketball court. When he was playing on the school team at St. Aloyisius, his coach offered to open up the school gym at 6:00 A.M. for anyone who wanted extra practice before school. John Stockton showed up every day.

But even that was not enough basketball for him. Sometimes, with friends, he would sneak into the large gym at Gonzaga University just four blocks away from home for pickup games. When he could not find an open gym, he wore out the family basketball net. John's long hours on the driveway court put him in top condition. As an eighth grader at St. Aloyisius, he set the school record for the mile run.

When Stockton moved on to Gonzaga Prep School, he continued his tireless practice habits. He shot baskets in his driveway day and night, in the summer rain and the winter snow.

The one thing Stockton's work habits could not improve, however, was his size. He stood only five feet five inches and weighed ninety pounds when he reported for practice as a freshman. But after so many years of competing against an older brother, John had grown used to his size disadvantage.

He was encouraged by the example of Gus Williams. Williams started as guard for John's favorite pro team, the Seattle Supersonics, during Stockton's high school days. Although not much over six feet tall, Williams led Seattle to

Stockton's boyhood hero, Gus Williams, penetrates the defense and then zips a pass to an open teammate.

the NBA title in 1979. The three-time All-Star averaged more than 23 points a game during his best season. While playing on his driveway court, Stockton would imagine that he was Gus Williams. He would picture himself weaving between the slower, taller players firing jump shots over their outstretched arms.

John got a first-hand look at his basketball hero when the Supersonics played an exhibition game in Spokane. Stockton was chosen to be the team's honorary ball boy for the night. Most who knew of Stockton's dream of playing in the NBA expected that this would be the closest he would ever come to achieving that dream.

Stockton, however, kept up his relentless pursuit of that dream. His work habits quickly earned him playing time at Gonzaga Prep ahead of older, larger, and stronger athletes. His dedication to basketball impressed one of his high school rivals—Mark Rypien. Rypien was such a committed athlete that he later quarterbacked the Washington Redskins to a Super Bowl title. Yet, even he was amazed at Stockton's incredible drive to succeed. "I remember driving by his house in high school at ten or eleven o'clock at night, and he was always out on the driveway, dribbling a basketball," Rypien said.

Stockton staged some memorable battles with Rypien, who starred for Shadle High School in Spokane. In one game against Rypien, Stockton scored 42 points for the Gonzaga Prep Bulldogs. But as would so often be the case, Stockton's play was overshadowed. It was Rypien who became Spokane's high school basketball hero. Not only did he lead Shadle to the state championship, but he set a tournament record for assists.

By his senior year at Gonzaga Prep, Stockton had grown to six feet. While he welcomed the improvement, he was still

16

short even for a high school basketball player. Stockton's boyish facial features made him appear even younger and smaller than he was. College scouts who watched him play had trouble believing he could match up against larger, stronger college athletes. Even many coaches who admired Stockton's ball-handling skills and enthusiasm did not want to risk a basketball scholarship on him.

In 1980, though, Stockton did receive a full scholarship offer from the college down the street. Gonzaga University was the third in the chain of Catholic schools that the Stockton family had attended for several generations. "I never consciously thought about going through the 'Gonzaga farm system,' but that's the way it happened," he recalls.

The Stocktons had done well at Gonzaga. John's grandfather had once been a football star at the school. But

The Gonzaga University campus where several generations of Stocktons received their degrees. The university's most famous alumnus is singer-entertainer Bing Crosby.

17

John knew that being a good athlete at Gonzaga was not the same as being a star at a major state university. Gonzaga served little more than three thousand students. It's most famous alumnus was not an athlete, but singer-entertainer Bing Crosby. Few sports fans across the nation had ever heard of Gonzaga. Nor would they hear of John Stockton for the next four years.

Yet Stockton found advantages to playing at a small, out-of-the-way school. The most important of these was playing time. Had he attended a major basketball power such as Duke or Indiana, he would have spent at least the first couple of years on the bench. Thereafter, he would have had to fight a deep roster of top athletes for a starting position.

Gonzaga, however, did not attract a host of top athletes. Stockton was able to work his way into the lineup from the beginning. He learned on the job how to play against skilled opponents. At the same time, he never slacked off in his practice habits. Gradually, his long hours in the practice gym began to pay off. Stockton improved each season.

One year, Steve Kerr, a high school basketball hotshot from Los Angeles, showed an interest in attending Gonzaga. The Gonzaga coaches encouraged the promising, young point guard to show what he could do in a practice session against the team's point guard. Having never heard of John Stockton, Kerr welcomed the challenge. Stockton then proceeded to run circles around Kerr. He stole the ball, slashed past Kerr for layups, grabbed loose balls, and fired jump shots with hair-trigger quickness. By the time practice was over, Kerr was thoroughly discouraged. Stockton did not seem to be particularly quick. If Kerr could be so thoroughly whipped by an unknown, skinny kid from a place called Gonzaga, how could he hope to play college basketball? Gonzaga coaches seemed to be thinking the same thing—they did not offer him a scholarship.

None of them was aware of what a tough test Kerr had faced. Once Kerr recovered from the experience, he proved himself good enough to earn All-American honors for the powerhouse University of Arizona. He was talented enough to go on to join the pro ranks. But, coming out of high school, he just was not good enough to handle John Stockton.

Stockton earned a solid reputation among coaches in the West Coast Athletic Conference. During his senior year, he led the league in scoring, assists, and steals. Stockton was voted the league's Most Valuable Player for the 1983-84 season.

Such accomplishments did not necessarily impress basketball experts. Anyone can look good playing against weak opposition. But the United States Olympic basketball officials wanted to leave no stone unturned in their search for the top college basketball players in the country. Every so often, a small college player blossoms into a star. So the Olympic coaches invited Stockton and several other lesser-known players from small schools to the Olympic tryout.

Well-known players such as Michael Jordan captured most of the attention at the tryouts. Yet after a few days, observers started noticing the pesky little waterbug from Gonzaga. Stockton was making the most of his one opportunity to match up against the big stars. He was beating opponents to the ball, slashing past them on the dribble, and shredding their defense with crisp passes.

Competition for the twelve spots on the team was fierce. Such overpowering college players as Charles Barkley and Karl Malone failed to make the team. Yet when U.S. Olympic coach Bob Knight trimmed the team to twenty players,

Stockton was one of the players he kept. Stockton lasted until the final cut, when Coach Knight reluctantly let him go.

But even though Stockton failed in his bid to make the Olympic team, the trials were the best thing to happen to his basketball career. A host of pro scouts had been watching the trials, and every one came away impressed with John Stockton. Some of them thought that Stockton not only should have made the team, but that he had outplayed every other point guard in the camp.

For the first time, important basketball people believed that Stockton might possibly be pro material.

Chapter 3

One of those who studied Stockton's Olympic tryout performance was Utah Jazz scout Jack Gardner. The more Gardner watched, the more he became convinced that this small, slender kid had the look of a winner.

In the spring of 1984, the Utah Jazz were not looking for a point guard. They already had a good one in former Michigan All-American Rickey Green. Yet Gardner insisted that the Jazz could not afford to pass up Stockton. He was willing to stake his reputation as a scout that Stockton would be a star.

After hearing the glowing report from their scout, the Jazz hoped for two things: 1) that Gardner was right; and 2) that other teams had not come to the same conclusion. The Jazz did their best to keep Stockton a secret. In the weeks before the draft, they avoided mentioning him as a possible choice. As a result, their choice of Stockton in the first round caught Utah fans off guard.

As much as they liked their new prospect, even the Jazz did not realize how dedicated a player Stockton was. While contract negotiations prevented him from joining the team right away, Stockton was not about to let the time go to waste. He asked the Jazz for videos of the team so that he could study the way the team played offense and defense. Stockton paid close attention to Rickey Green's duties.

Stockton's homework paid off. When he finally reported to the Jazz, Stockton stunned coaches with his knowledge of Utah's system. From day one, the rookie could direct the offense as if he had been playing in Utah for years.

Stockton believes this type of intense preparation was another positive result of his playing at a small college. He never felt that he could afford to relax and coast on his success, not even for a second. When he unexpectedly found himself claimed as a first-round draft choice, the success did not go to his head. According to Stockton, when you come

Rickey Green averaged 13.2 points and 9.2 assists as Utah's starting point guard in 1983-84, the year before Stockton arrived.

from a small college, "You know you're an underdog. And when you start to achieve some good results, you still keep that underdog attitude."

Stockton impressed Utah coach Frank Layden with his competitiveness, his quickness, his large, fast hands, his endurance, and especially his dribbling ability. Stockton could dribble well with either hand. He could squirt through and zip around a double-team as easily as if he had the ball on a string. Stockton was the perfect weapon against teams that liked to put on a full-court press in hopes of forcing a turnover. "John's dribbling skills make us practically press-proof," said coach Layden.

Stockton's small-town, underdog attitude endeared him to Utah fans. Some star players were reluctant to play for Utah. The team was located in the NBA's smallest population center, and so Jazz players seldom got as much press coverage and recognition as other players. Stockton, though, did not care about press coverage. He never read articles about himself for fear they would distract him. He let Utah fans know that he preferred Salt Lake City to the larger metropolitan areas.

One thing that Stockton was not used to was sitting on the bench. But he had to face the fact that Rickey Green was in his prime and playing well. Stockton, for all his enthusiasm and dedication, was still a very small player who was very new to the pro game. He needed to focus his energy and not play out of control, especially on defense. Stockton had a habit of chasing guys all over the court, constantly trying for a steal. This sometimes left him out of position and allowed the opposition to score easily. He had to learn to pick his spots when trying for a steal.

During his rookie season, Stockton found himself on the bench more often than not. Although he appeared in every

Jazz game, he averaged only 5.6 points and 5.1 assists per game. Those were not exactly the kind of numbers fans expected from a top draft choice. The addition of Stockton certainly did not bring the team closer to a championship. In fact, the Jazz slumped to a 41-41 mark that year. Their record was barely good enough to make the play-offs, where they fell to Denver in the second round.

Stockton's second season was not much better. Utah improved by the barest of margins, to 42-40. Stockton, still playing a supporting role to Rickey Green, averaged 7.7 points and 7.4 assists per game.

Beneath the surface, however, Stockton showed signs of better things to come. He protected the ball as well as anyone in the game. He played tenacious defense and averaged more than two steals per game. Best of all, he showed he could rise to a challenge. When Stockton took the court against Magic Johnson, the best guard in the world at the time, he refused to be awed. Instead, he played his finest game of the season, dealing out 17 assists.

Stockton demonstates the skills that make his team "press-proof."

Notice that Stockton never looks at the ball while dribbling, no matter which hand he uses.

The best thing to happen to Stockton in his second season was the arrival of Karl Malone. Malone, a power forward from Louisiana Tech, was Stockton's opposite in almost every way. Stockton was a white man from the urban North, Malone a black man from the rural South. Stockton grew up in a comfortable middle class household and was close to his father. Malone's father was not that close. Karl's mother worked in a sawmill, struggling to support her nine children.

Stockton had no colorful nickname. He shunned the spotlight and rarely spoke to reporters. Malone was known throughout the country as "The Mailman." He was a flashy, outgoing man who loved to perform in front of people. Stockton enjoyed being an ordinary, everyday person. Malone had a taste for the unusual. For example, he kept a house full of huge pet snakes. Malone psyched himself into bursts of rage, during which he charged around like an angry bull.

Their most important difference was physical. While Stockton had to overcome a size handicap, Malone was "the most awesomely constructed individual who has ever played basketball," according to *Sport* magazine. He stood 6 feet 9 inches and weighed 260 pounds. He had a granite-like chest, enormous shoulders, and arms like sledgehammers. When that huge man of steel roared downcourt at full speed, a path usually opened up for him. According to one NBA player, "People tend to get out of Karl's way unless they want their careers to be over."

The one thing that Malone could not do very well was dribble the ball into position to score. He needed someone to get him the ball near the basket where he could use his strength, or out in the clear where he could launch his deadly jump shot. It just so happened that John Stockton could pass the ball as well as any guard in the game. Stockton and Malone began to see that their skills complemented each other

Utah's selection of Louisiana Tech star Karl Malone brought more applause than did the team's choice of Stockton the previous year.

perfectly. If Stockton could get the ball down the court and set up Malone for the shot, the Mailman would deliver.

The Malone-Stockton connection took several years before it fired on all cylinders. Both players had much to learn before they could become a force in the league. Stockton, while he had demonstrated he could be a solid role player, had given no indication that he would become a star. Free-throw shooting proved to be the chink in Malone's armor. He missed more than half his foul shots during his rookie season.

In his third year as a pro, Stockton still could not win a starting job in the Utah lineup. He continued to average fewer than 8 points a game and had trouble hitting long-range shots. He boosted his assists, however, to 8.2 per game and his steals to better than 2 per game. Both figures ranked in the top 10 in the NBA despite Stockton's limited playing time.

By the end of that year, Utah coaches were thinking that Stockton might be ready to take over as the starting point guard. When Rickey Green suffered an injury at the end of the season, Stockton got the chance to run the club in the play-offs. He did a respectable job as the Jazz lost to Golden State in the first round.

The Stockton-Malone era of Utah Jazz history started the following season—1987-88. In the fourth game of the year, Utah turned over the offense to Stockton. He responded like a root-bound plant suddenly transplanted into good soil. The more minutes per game he played, the better he got—in all phases of the game. He could thread passes through a forest of waving arms and slither through a lane crowded with big bodies. When defenders sagged back to protect against his passes, he showed that he could bury the long jump shot. On defense, he would jab at the ball and knock it free, then outrace the opposition to the loose ball.

Stockton took advantage of the discovery that big Karl Malone loved to attack the basket on the run. This required long passes made on the run, the most dangerous passes in the NBA. If they do not sail out of bounds, they are often intercepted by pros who are fast enough to catch up to any ball that hangs in the air. But Stockton seemed to have a computer in his head that instantly calculated where and when to throw the ball and at what speed.

Utah Jazz highlight films were soon filled with Stockton-to-Malone clips. Their trademark was a long, line-drive pass from Stockton to a sprinting Malone, followed by a thunderous slam dunk. With Stockton as his setup man, Malone gained a reputation as the best running big man in history.

In his first year as a starter, Stockton ended Magic Johnson's quest for a fifth assist title in six years. On April 12, 1988, he collected his 1,000th assist of the year in a game against the Los Angeles Clippers. Only two other players in NBA history had gone over 1,000 assists in a season. Later that week, Stockton put on a passing clinic for the Portland Trail Blazers. His 26 assists was the highest assist total by an NBA player in six years.

Meanwhile, Karl Malone had sharpened his free-throw shooting skills. Combined with his aggressive moves to the basket, the third-year forward scored nearly 27 points per game. Only Michael Jordan scored at a faster clip than Malone that season.

With Stockton scoring, passing, and defending, Malone scoring, rebounding, and drawing fouls, and seven-foot four-inch center Mark Eaton blocking shots, Utah won a franchise record 47 games.

Stockton more than fulfilled the hopes Utah had for him when they had drafted him in 1984. He finished the season with 1,128 assists. That broke the NBA mark of 1,123 held by Detroit's Isiah Thomas. Stockton's 242 steals ranked third in the league. He nearly doubled his scoring average with 14.7 points a game.

Perhaps the most surprising feat of all, was his shooting accuracy. In his three seasons as a reserve, Stockton didn't make half his shots and sank fewer than 20 percent of his three-point shots. But once he was given the starting job, he responded with radar accuracy. His 57 percent shooting was almost unheard of for an NBA guard who plays far away from the basket. He nearly doubled his accuracy from behind the three-point line to 35 percent.

The Stockton-Malone combination at work against the Boston Celtics. Stockton draws a crowd and passes to a wide-open Malone.

With numbers like that, the last lingering doubts that Stockton belonged in the pros dissolved. Hometown fans of little John Stockton wondered how many more surprises this determined young man had in store. It so happened that Stockton had a huge surprise waiting in the play-offs for Magic Johnson and the powerful Los Angeles Lakers.

Chapter 4

The Utah Jazz had enjoyed little play-off success during Stockton's first three years. Heading into the 1988 postseason, they had lost their last 3 play-off series by a total of 10 games to 4.

Utah broke the streak by taking 3 of 4 games from Portland. Unfortunately, their victory sent them against the Los Angeles Lakers in round two. Led by stylish guard Magic Johnson, silky-smooth forward James Worthy, and the ultimate scoring machine, Kareem Abdul-Jabbar, the run-and-gun Lakers had posted the best record in the league. They were heavily favored to win the championship.

For once, John Stockton would take center stage in an important national contest. More often than most pro teams, the Lakers and Jazz depended on their point guards to run the offense. Stockton had taken away Magic Johnson's title as the NBA's top assist man, now he would have to battle the superstar head to head.

Johnson and the Lakers came out blazing. From the opening tap, they shut down the Jazz attack. Utah scored only

8 points in the first quarter. Meanwhile, the Lakers ran through the Jazz as though their home court was an express lane on the freeway. Los Angeles raced to a 55-31 lead at halftime. They toyed with the Jazz the rest of the way as they romped to a 110-91 victory.

The Lakers' Magic Show was so devastating that Utah's coach was moved to say what no coach is ever supposed to admit. "I don't think we can beat the Lakers," said Coach Frank Layden.

Stockton and the Jazz, however, were not ready to throw in the towel. Far from being intimidated by Magic Johnson's reputation, Stockton welcomed the challenge of matching skills with the best. In game two, young John Stockton gave the master a lesson in how to play point guard. Stockton set up teammates for scores 13 times. At the same time, he protected the ball well, turning the ball over only 3 times against one of the league's top defenses. Johnson, on the other hand, collected 10 assists while losing the ball 8 times.

Utah's huge center, Mark Eaton, disrupted the Lakers' offense by blocking 7 shots. Karl Malone burned the Lakers defense for 29 points. With Stockton chipping in 19 points of his own, Utah stunned Los Angeles, 101-97, on the Lakers' home court.

The Lakers appeared to have treated the Jazz too lightly after their easy first-game win. Now that Utah had embarrassed the Lakers in front of their home fans, most experts expected Los Angeles to bounce back in game three.

But with Stockton directing a patient, disciplined attack, Utah broke out to an early lead. Every time Los Angeles would mount a rally, Stockton answered it with a crisp pass, a steal, or a score of his own. The Jazz never trailed in the contest. Stockton so thoroughly outplayed Johnson that the Lakers' coach took Magic out of the game in the fourth

In his first year as a starter, Stockton found himself locked in fierce competition with the point guard he most admired, Magic Johnson.

quarter. Never before in his career had Johnson been benched in the fourth quarter of a play-off game. Utah claimed the victory, 96-89, with Stockton contributing 22 points and 12 assists.

It was a grim Los Angeles team that entered Utah's Salt Palace for game four of the series. The Lakers, so confident and dominating just a week earlier, were fighting to stay alive. For years, they had enjoyed a huge advantage at the point guard position in almost every game they played. With Stockton patrolling the floor, however, that advantage was gone. If they lost this game, the Lakers would fall behind three games to one in the best-of-seven series. Few teams had ever come back from such a deficit.

With Stockton slashing to the basket and threading precise passes to his teammates, the Jazz again frustrated the talented Lakers. Utah controlled the first half and then built their lead up to nine points in the third quarter. At that point, though, Mark Eaton got into foul trouble. Utah did not have experienced front line reserves to back him up. Without Eaton clogging the middle of the lane, the Lakers drove toward the basket at will. They pulled out the victory despite Stockton's 13 assists.

The series shifted back to Los Angeles. Even on their home court, though, the Lakers could not manhandle the pesky Jazz. John Stockton played like a man possessed. Refusing to leave the game for even a moment's rest, he led charge after charge on the Lakers' net. When he wasn't firing laser passes through a clutter of bodies to a waiting teammate, he was driving the Lakers crazy with his dribbling. He repeatedly threw the Lakers' offense out of rhythm by stealing the ball or harassing the Los Angeles guards.

Despite Stockton's efforts, the Lakers' talented veterans also came through with clutch performances. By the middle of the fourth quarter, they had forged a 90-84 lead and were ready to put the game away. But Stockton was not through yet. With almost impossible accuracy, he zipped passes through the heart of the Laker defense. Taking advantage of the close-range scoring chances that Stockton provided, Utah closed the gap. With less than a minute to go, the Jazz took the lead.

By that time, John Stockton had poured out his heart on the floor. Because Utah called on him to handle the ball so much, he had to work harder than anyone else on the floor, yet he had played every second of the game. He had tied Magic Johnson's single game play-off record of 24 assists. Stockton had also scored 23 points and had come up with 5 steals.

Yet all that effort went to waste in the final twelve seconds. Los Angeles put on a final flurry to win, 111-109.

Disappointed but not discouraged, the Jazz headed back home for game six. This time they left the Lakers no chance for a last-second escape. They drilled almost all their shots in a first-quarter flurry. Utah overwhelmed the Lakers, 26-2, during that spurt to put the game out of reach almost as soon as it started. Stockton dealt out 17 assists, scored 14 points, and recorded 3 steals in Utah's 108-80 win.

That set the stage for the seventh and final game at Los Angeles. Magic Johnson thrived on that kind of pressure. He rose to the challenge by playing his finest game of the series. Johnson dished out 16 assists and scored 23 points, many of them at crucial times.

Yet even with this fine performance, Johnson could not quite keep up with the pace of his lesser-known opponent. Stockton notched 20 assists. When the Lakers clamped down on his teammates, Stockton stepped up to deliver key baskets. He kept the Jazz close for much of the game with his 29 points. But Magic Johnson had a more talented supporting

Although famous for his passing, Stockton has proved that he can hit the open jump shot.

Despite his success, Stockton continues to work hard on all the basic skills, including free-throw shooting.

pro stars. "I can't get away with trying to be tricky," he admitted. So while many other stars worked on crowd-pleasing, gravity-defying offensive moves, Stockton kept polishing his basic skills.

Stockton also accepted the fact that he was most effective as a point guard when he got his teammates involved in the offense. He knew that the Jazz would not be a successful team if he tried to be the scoring star. They could not win with John Stockton trying to outscore the other team by himself, but they could win if he worked hard to help his teammates get the best shots possible.

Again, Stockton credited his experience as an unknown player from a small, unheralded college for helping him play unselfishly. "Having gone to Gonzaga, you learn humility," he explained. "My feet are firmly on the ground."

The most important reason why Stockton managed to avoid superstar recognition was because of his personality. According to Jerry Sloan, who took over as head coach of the Jazz from Frank Layden, many pro players work hard on making a name for themselves. "Other guys get their reputations because they build themselves up by overpromoting themselves."

Stockton was different. "I've never been one to like being in focus," Stockton says. He rarely had much to say to the press on any subject. He especially hated talking about himself.

Stockton came by his humble traits naturally. Over the years, his father's friends often wanted to decorate Jack & Dan's bar with pictures of John in his Utah uniform. Although Jack was enormously proud of his son's accomplishments, he never allowed the photographs. He made it plain that the Stocktons don't believe in blowing their own horns.

Stockton threads the needle with a no-look bounce pass.

Similarly, John had no interest in acting like he was more important than others. He was not into the fast-living, money-spending style of many wealthy celebrities. Even though he could have made a great deal of money in Utah and Spokane by endorsing products, he rarely got involved in commercials and public appearances.

That did not mean that Stockton was aloof from other players or that he looked down on them. In fact, he enjoyed getting to know other pro basketball players. He disagreed with critics who claimed that friendliness among pro players should be discouraged because athletes might not play their hardest against good friends.

"I don't think you're looking your buddy in the eye when you're playing," he responded. "It's just a body out there. From a personal standpoint, you would waste a tremendous opportunity to meet some great people if you just turned your back on everyone."

But Stockton has probably succeeded more than any other top player in living his life unchanged by NBA success. Instead of buying himself a new mansion with his large NBA salary, he bought an old house next door to his parents in Spokane. Instead of hiring someone to restore the place, Stockton spent part of his summers working as his own handyman. How many top NBA stars can be found hanging from a roof with their tool belts, pounding new siding into place?

John lived at the house with his wife, Nada, a hometown girl with whom he attended school at Gonzaga. When they started a family, John became even more concerned about preserving his privacy. He did not want his wife and children to be freaks in the media show that often trails pro athletes. Jazz teammates noted that once Stockton's three children began to arrive, he became even more reluctant to appear in public or to allow reporters to interview him. He bought a remote cabin an hour away from Spokane as a getaway place where he and his family would not be bothered.

But while he wanted to shield his family from gawking eyes, Stockton was not about to cut himself off from his old friends and neighbors. He was determined not to turn his back on the people who had supported him all these years. Stockton frequently visited old coaches and teammates. He set up and ran a basketball camp for youngsters in Spokane who had the same love for basketball that had driven him to the pros. Many pro teams forbid their stars from playing basketball outside team practices and games, for fear of injury. But Stockton insisted that the Jazz write a clause into his contract that allowed him to play summer league basketball games with his old buddies. He also likes to play in a summer softball league with the guys.

Throughout his years as a pro, Stockton has continued to act as though he were still the underdog from Gonzaga who was thrilled to have a chance to play against the big stars in the NBA. If he has not received as much publicity as players with less ability, he could not care less. He never expected it and never wanted it. Stockton enjoys playing basketball and he wants to win at it as badly as he always has. But he has never cared much for fame. John Stockton is not a nationally known superstar simply because he chooses not to be one.

Steve Stockton summed up his brother's attitude toward his success as a pro basketball player by saying, "He never holds anything over your head. When the season's over, he comes home and that's it."

Chapter 6

Mention John Stockton's name among pro fans, and someone will automatically bring up Karl Malone. Talk about Malone, and someone is certain to mention Stockton. Since the two rose to success at the same time with the same team, their names have been linked as if they were twins. "Mr. Inside and Mr. Outside" meshed their skills better than any other duo in the league. They were the two opposites who, with a very weak supporting cast, made the Utah Jazz a title contender every season.

Their close association has been a mixed blessing for both players. On the one hand, having two great players on the same team has watered down the impact of each of them. Instead of one star to rally around in Utah, fans and the press had to split attention between two. Stockton and Malone have worked together so well that it has been almost impossible to decide which of the two was more important to the team. Several basketball experts believe that this fact prevents either Stockton or Malone from winning the league's Most Valuable Player award. If neither was clearly the most valuable member

Utah's Dynamic Duo.

of their team, how could either be considered the most valuable in the NBA? Utah supporters would always split their vote between the two stars, and the award would go to someone else.

When it came to attracting fan recognition, Stockton paled next to the huge, handsome, outgoing Mailman. Far more fans pay attention to rebounding and scoring statistics than to assists. Malone dominated these areas. He was the first NBA forward to average more than 30 points and 10 rebounds per game since the great Elgin Baylor had managed the feat 27 years before. Had Michael Jordan not been in the league at the same time as Malone, Karl would have led the NBA in scoring four straight seasons. Stockton's quiet, serious expression on the court and his heads-up precision could not compete with the monster slam dunks, high point totals, and fist-pumping emotion of Utah's Mailman.

On the other hand, neither Stockton nor Malone minded being paired with the other in the public eye. They are friends who hold enormous respect for each other.

"Karl Malone is one of the best finishers in the game," Stockton has said. He was quick to admit that many of his assists have been due to Malone's skill. Once Malone received a pass, the big guy found a way to put the ball in the basket.

Malone was equally impressed with Stockton. "He's the smartest player I have ever known," Malone said of his teammate. Malone knew from personal experience how cagey Stockton could be. One time the Jazz were stuck in a losing streak and playing poorly. Their next game was on the road in Charlotte, against the Hornets.

While the Jazz were shooting their pregame warm-ups, Stockton sidled up to Malone. He mentioned that he had been watching a local Charlotte sports station the previous night.

Basketball's best finisher, Karl Malone is strong enough to score even with a giant Shaq on his back.

One of the players, said Stockton, had scoffed that Karl Malone was not as good a player as most people claimed.

Stockton's words lit a fire under the proud Malone. Malone stormed onto the court, determined to show the doubting Hornets that the Mailman was the real thing. Malone spent the entire evening knocking around the Hornets and slamming the ball through the rim. By the time he was finished, he had poured in 52 points! Led by Malone's ferocious performance, Utah easily beat Charlotte and snapped their losing streak. After the game, Malone explained why he had been so motivated for the game. Only then did the truth come out. None of the Hornets had said anything negative about Malone. Stockton had made up the story to get Malone riled up to play his best game of the season.

Malone appreciated Stockton so much that he became very protective of his teammate. Because of his small size, Stockton was often an easy target for a flying elbow or a hard shove. Malone would have none of it. "Anyone messes with

"Don't even think about stealing!"

48

Stockton has no trouble playing keep-away from defenders while calculating where to fire his next pass.

Stockton messes with me," he announced.

Malone also grew irritated with fans for not recognizing Stockton's skills. One year, fans voted Malone to the Western Division's starting All-Star lineup but passed over Stockton in favor of another point guard. An angry Malone threatened to sit out the All-Star game. At the very least, he would wear Stockton's number 12 in his honor. The All-Star coaches, however, cooled Malone's wrath by adding Stockton to the team as a reserve.

The annual All-Star game turned out to be the most dazzling showcase of the Stockton-Malone connection. In the 1989 game, Stockton and Malone spent the first quarter playing pitch-and-catch high above the Eastern Conference's defenders. Battling against some of the top players in the world, Stockton collected more assists in one quarter (9) than most pro point guards get in an entire game against normal opposition.

Stockton finished the game with 17 assists to go along with 11 points. Malone scored 28 points and grabbed 9 rebounds. The two Utah stars so dominated the contest that the Most Valuable Player award had to go to one of them. Stockton had to take a back seat as usual, as Malone edged him out in the voting.

Utah's dynamic duo topped that performance four years later in front of a deafening home crowd at Salt Lake City's new Delta Center. The game proved far more intense than the usual free-wheeling, high-scoring All-Star exhibition. New stars such as Shaquille O'Neal and Larry Johnson welcomed the chance to show they deserved their press clippings. The established stars were equally determined to show these millionaire rookies who was still boss in the NBA.

Again, Stockton and Malone blew out of the starting blocks so fast that they left the Eastern Conference in the dust. Stockton fired a bounce pass past his defender to Malone, who was cutting toward the basket. Slam dunk! Stockton lofted a lob toward the basket. Malone soared high above the rim to grab it. Slam dunk! Four times in the first quarter alone, Stockton set up the Mailman for easy shots and rim-shaking dunks. He added 3 assists to other Western stars.

But the Eastern stars, led by Michael Jordan and Patrick Ewing, regrouped. Before long, the game turned into a furious struggle. Malone kept the Western team in the game with his scoring and rebounding, Stockton with his passing.

The teams fought to a tie at the end of regulation time. Then the splendidly conditioned Stockton took over. With the West clinging to a narrow lead in the final minute, Stockton slapped the ball away from Cleveland's Mark Price and raced downcourt. He then buried a jump shot to clinch the 135-132 victory.

Again, All-Star officials faced an almost impossible choice in their balloting for Most Valuable Player. Malone had dominated the front court. He had sunk 11 of 17 shots, scored 28 points, and snared 10 rebounds. Stockton had dominated the back court. He had totaled 15 assists, and had broken open the game with 4 crucial points and a steal in overtime. This time, the voters could not choose between the two. They gave the MVP award to both Stockton and Malone.

For once, Stockton could not avoid standing at center stage, fielding questions from the press. Typically, he turned the attention away from himself. "There were a lot of young guys who wanted to go out there and win as bad as anything," he said. "I think Shaq, Larry Johnson, and everyone in the so-called older group was competing very hard so it made it a lot of fun."

Those who knew Stockton well, knew that this was not just false modesty. For Stockton, the thrill of the competition really did mean more than the award.

Chapter 7

Despite his reluctant nature, John Stockton had one other golden chance to make a splash on the national sports scene. In 1992, United States Olympic officials agreed to allow professionals to represent the country in basketball competition at the Olympics in Barcelona, Spain. Sports fans buzzed over the idea of a Dream Team—the best players from the pros all playing in a USA uniform. Imagine Magic Johnson, Michael Jordan, Larry Bird, David Robinson, Charles Barkley, Karl Malone, Clyde Drexler, Jeff Mullin, and Patrick Ewing all on the same team!

When the selection committee announced the eleven pro players who had been chosen for the Dream Team, all those familiar names were on the list. Only one name on the list caused murmuring and grumbling: John Stockton.

Stockton's selection especially surprised people on the East Coast, half a continent away from the small market in which he played. Many complained that Detroit's Isiah Thomas should have been chosen instead.

Had they studied the record books, fans would have found ample evidence that this small, relatively unknown Jazz player was the best point guard in the NBA. In his five years as a starter prior to the Olympics, Stockton had led the NBA in assists every season. In three of those seasons, he had set a new league record for assists.

On closer inspection, the record clearly showed that pro basketball had never seen a passer and floor leader quite like him. In the previous history of the NBA, only two players had managed to collect 1,000 assists in a season. Kevin Porter had done it first for the Detroit Pistons in 1978-79. Isiah Thomas had accomplished the feat in 1984-85. Stockton, however, had gone over 1,000 assists *five years in a row*.

While some fans and sportswriters questioned Stockton's fitness to be on the team, NBA players and coaches lined up on the Utah guard's side. They were far more appreciative than fans of the little, unnoticed things that Stockton did to win games.

"When you get Stockton to turn the ball over, it's almost a badge of honor," said one coach.

No one appreciates the fine art of point guard play more than Bob Cousy, the brilliant guard who led the Boston Celtics to titles in the 1950s and 60s. He noted that every season the Jazz were among the NBA leaders in percentage of shots made. That, said Cousy, was largely because of Stockton's ability to penetrate the defense and to find the open man with a pass that would set them up for good shots.

No one appreciated Stockton more than his coach, Jerry Sloan. "He's mentally prepared every single moment," said Sloan. "John can let guys cross and go through the middle and all of a sudden, bang, something happens for him." What happens is that Stockton sizes up the situation before anyone else.

Although he is only six foot one inch, the determined Stockton soars above other players on the court. His talent and league records earned him a spot on the first Dream Team.

Sloan marveled at Stockton's uncanny ability to find a narrow shaft of space in a congested area. When Sloan was asked to compare Stockton to Guy Rodgers, who had played with Sloan and was considered one of the finest passers of his time, Sloan said, "Rodgers could do it in the open court, but I don't think he could pick people out in a congested area the way John can."

The questioning of Stockton's selection for the Dream Team was ironic. Eight years earlier he had been denied a spot on the Olympic team that many felt he deserved. When he finally made the Olympic team, people were saying that he did not deserve it. The controversy enraged Karl Malone, who called it "a disgrace." Stockton simply shrugged off the fuss. "I can't help what other people think, so I don't worry about it," he said.

Coach Sloan confirmed that Stockton was not losing any sleep over criticism of his selection. "He's not concerned about any of that stuff, because all he wants to do is compete."

The Dream Team gave Stockton a chance to team up with his old rival, Magic Johnson, as the USA's other main point guard. The offense they led was so talented that their competition stood in awe of them. In the Tournament of the Americas, which was the qualifying round for the Olympics, the USA flattened the opposition like a tank running over ripe fruit. The Cuban players were thrilled just to be able to meet the American stars. Before the game, some of them asked if the Americans would pose with them for photographs so they could show the folks back home. The Americans obliged and then crushed the Cubans, 136-57, on the court. Canada's center Bill Wennington summed up the feeling of most of the world when he said, "The world will end before the USA is beaten."

Although the heat of competition that Stockton loved was missing, he continued to work hard in practice and go all out in games. "I think we owe it to ourselves and the other teams to keep playing and not let up," he said. The Dream Team followed Stockton's example. It did not let up during the Tournament of the Americas. In qualifying for the Olympics, it trounced its opponents by an average margin of more than 51 points!

Simply by being one of the Dream Team, Stockton was winning more public praise and recognition than ever before. But, as usual, something happened to prevent him from reaping his true share of credit. During the team's 44-point romp over Canada, Michael Jordan accidently kicked Stockton in the leg. Stockton limped off the court with a fractured bone while the Dream Team dissolved into a nightmare for him.

The only cure for the injury was rest. Stockton had to watch from the sidelines as the Dream Team routed one opponent after another. A less competitive man might have given up and watched the rest of the Olympics in street clothes, but Stockton badly wanted to play in the Olympics.

Although not totally healed, he rejoined the team in time for the final four games. He managed to play a few minutes in each game, including the team's gold-medal victory over Croatia.

The world did not get to see the true John Stockton. He could not slither past defenders into the lane or deal out assists like a dealer in a blackjack game. In 29 total minutes of play on a tender leg, he still managed to score 11 points and contribute 8 assists. But when he walked up to collect his gold medal, he remained the least-recognized player of America's Dream Team.

Chapter 8

John Stockton no longer has to scratch and claw for his place among the thoroughbreds of pro basketball. Even if he never plays another second for the Utah Jazz, his place as one of the NBA's most brilliant point guards is secure.

Ever since Stockton broke into the Jazz lineup, the race for the NBA assist title among other players has been for second place. In 1993-94, Stockton claimed the title for the seventh straight year. As usual, no one came close to challenging him. He was poised to break Magic Johnson's all-time assist record of 9,921 before the next season was out. Johnson compiled that mark in twelve seasons as a starter. Stockton passed it in only his eleventh year in the pros, his eighth as a starter.

There is a better than even chance that Stockton's large, cobra-quick hands will create more steals than anyone else in NBA history. Although he looks for his shot only after all other options are closed, he has averaged better than 15 points per game over his starting career. Despite having to launch most of his shots from long range, and over giants, he has made more than half of his attempts.

Stockton burst through play-off rival Portland for a layup.

Stockton has earned recognition as a first-team All-Pro. Hall of Famer Wilt Chamberlain has said that if he were building a pro team from scratch, he would start with Stockton. Former pro guard Rod Hundley, who has seen such greats as Cousy and Rodgers in action says, "I honestly believe he's the best true point guard ever to play the game."

Yet even at the height of his career, Stockton remained the scrappy little underdog from Gonzaga University. He showed up for every practice ready to work harder than anyone else. He asked for no special privileges or pampering. He never shied away from the grueling, even painful tasks that hardly anyone notices but which help a team win. At 175 pounds, Stockton is the last person you would expect to be setting screens to free up his teammates for shots. Yet he planted himself in the path of 275-pound bruisers so skillfully that one coach called him "the very best at the underappreciated art of screening."

Stockton's willingness to take a hit for the team scared his much larger friend, Karl Malone. "I worry about John down there getting whacked around by the guys who guard me," Malone said. "John takes them all on."

So far, Stockton's efforts have not brought Utah the NBA title that all pro players crave. In fact, the Jazz have been plagued by poor showings in post season. Many experts believe that Utah's problem is that they rely too heavily on Stockton and Malone to carry the load. In the play-offs, teams make a special effort to keep the ball out of Stockton's hands. They wear down the Jazz with their deeper rosters.

Stockton came closest to gaining the NBA finals in 1992. That year the Jazz edged the Los Angeles Clippers and then trounced Seattle in early play-off action. In the Western Conference finals, Stockton staged an exhausting duel with Portland point guard Terry Porter. "We're going to be exchanging each other's jerseys if we get any closer," Porter said in the middle of the series.

Utah and Portland each won two games of the best-of-seven series, setting the stage for the crucial fifth game. Utah carried the game into overtime on Portland's home court, only to lose a heartbreaker, 127-121. Portland went on to win the series in six games. The Jazz also came up short in the Western Conference finals against Houston in 1994.

Whether gaining individual success or suffering play-off disappointment, Stockton continues to battle, because it is the only way he knows how to play. He takes losing personally. And despite his record-setting feats, Stockton is always looking to improve. Even during his reign as the NBA's king of assists, Stockton pointed to Magic Johnson as his role

In an effort to lighten John Stockton's load and to end the team's play-off frustrations, the Utah Jazz traded for sharp-shooting Jeff Hornacek in 1993-94.

model. When the pressure was the greatest, Johnson could practically carry his team to victory on his shoulders. "I have to get to the point where I can do it like Magic does," he said.

Many people think it's good enough that he does it like John Stockton does. In the words of one admiring rival coach, "Every time I watch him, he leaves me scratching my head."

Career Statistics

COLLEGE

Year	Team	GP	FG%	REB	AST	PTS	AVG
1980-81	Gonzaga	25	.578	11	34	78	3.1
1981-82	Gonzaga	27	.576	67	135	303	11.2
1982-83	Gonzaga	27	.518	87	184	375	13.9
1983-84	Gonzaga	28	.577	66	201	584	20.9
Totals		107	.559	231	554	1,340	12.5

NBA

Year	Team	GP	FG%	REB	AST	STL	PTS	AVG
1984-85	Utah	82	.471	105	415	109	458	5.6
1985-86	Utah	82	.489	179	610	157	630	7.7
1986-87	Utah	82	.499	151	670	177	648	7.9
1987-88	Utah	82	.574	237	1,128	242	1,204	14.7
1988-89	Utah	82	.538	248	1,118	263	1,400	17.1
1989-90	Utah	78	.514	206	1,134	207	1,345	17.2
1990-91	Utah	82	.507	237	1,164	234	1,413	17.2
1991-92	Utah	82	.482	270	1,126	244	1,297	15.8
1992-93	Utah	82	.486	237	987	199	1,239	15.1
1993-94	Utah	82	.528	258	1,031	199	1,236	15.1
Totals		816	.512	2,128	9,383	2,031	10,870	13.3

Where to Write John Stockton

Mr. John Stockton
c/o Utah Jazz
Delta Center
301 West South Temple
Salt Lake City, UT 84101

Index

Porter, Kevin, 53
Porter, Terry, 60
Price, Mark, 50

R

Riley, Pat, 37
Robinson, David, 52
Rodgers, Guy, 55
Rypien, Mark, 15

S

St. Aloyisius Elementary School, 14, 15
Salt Lake City, 23
Salt Palace, 7, 9, 34
Sandberg, Ryne, 14
Shadle High School, 15
Sloan, Jerry, 40, 52, 55
Spokane, Washington, 13, 16, 42, 43
Sport, 26
Sports Illustrated, 12
Stockton, Clementine, 13
Stockton, Jack, 11, 13, 40
Stockton, John
   childhood, 13-17
   college, 17-19
   competition with Steve, 14
   dribbling skills, 23
   NBA All-Star games, 49-51
   NBA draft, 7-9, 21
   NBA starter, 27, 28
   Olympic team (1992), 52-56
   Olympic trials (1984), 19, 20
   passing skills, 50, 53, 55
   play-offs, 31-32, 34-37, 59-60
   private life, 38-40, 41-43
   records, 29, 35, 37, 53, 57

rookie season, 21-23
   with Karl Malone, 25-29, 45-51
Stockton, Nada, 42
Stockton, Steve, 14, 43

T

Thomas, Isiah, 29, 52
Tournament of the Americas, 55, 56
Tripucka, Kelly, 11

W

Wennington, Bill, 55
Williams, Gus, 15, 16
Willis, Kevin, 7
Worthy, James, 31, 37